First World War
and Army of Occupation
War Diary
France, Belgium and Germany

61 DIVISION
Divisional Troops
Divisional Cyclist Company
1 January 1915 - 31 January 1916

WO95/3042/1

The Naval & Military Press Ltd
www.nmarchive.com
Published in association with The National Archives

Published by

The Naval & Military Press Ltd

Unit 10 Ridgewood Industrial Park,

Uckfield, East Sussex,

TN22 5QE England

Tel: +44 (0) 1825 749494

www.naval-military-press.com

www.nmarchive.com

This diary has been reprinted in facsimile from the original. Any imperfections are inevitably reproduced and the quality may fall short of modern type and cartographic standards.

© **Crown Copyright**
Images reproduced by permission of The National Archives, London, England, 2015.

Contents

Document type	Place/Title	Date From	Date To
Heading	WO95/3042/1		
Heading	61 Division 61 Div Cyclist 1915 Nov-1916 Jan		
Miscellaneous	61st South Mid Division	08/10/1915	08/10/1915
Miscellaneous	1/8th (Cyclist) Bn. Essex Regt.	12/09/1915	12/09/1915
War Diary	Wickford	01/10/1915	03/10/1915
War Diary	Picknacre	04/10/1915	04/10/1915
War Diary	Billericay	05/10/1915	05/10/1915
War Diary	Wickford	05/10/1915	30/10/1915
Heading	War Diary of The 61st (S.M) Divl. Cyclist Coy From 1st Decr. To 31st Decr. 1915. Vol. 4.		
War Diary	Wickford	01/12/1915	31/12/1915
Heading	War Diary of 61st (S.M.) Divisional Cyclist Coy From 1st Jan 16, To 31st Jan 1916.		
War Diary	Wickford	01/01/1915	04/01/1915
War Diary	Wickford	05/01/1916	18/01/1916
War Diary	Burnham	19/01/1916	31/01/1916
Miscellaneous	Tactical Exercise 61st (Ser.) Divl Cyclist Coy. 6.1.16 Appendix "A"	06/01/1916	06/01/1916
Miscellaneous	Progress of Scheme.		
Miscellaneous	Tactical Exercise Tuesday 11.1.16 Appendix "B"	11/01/1916	11/01/1916

WO 95/3042/1

61 DIVISION

61 DIV CYCLIST

1915 NOV — 1916 JAN

WAR DIARY.

Unit: Cyclist Co (Divl Mounted Troops) 61st South Mid. Division
Brigade: —
Division: 61st South Mid Division
Mobilisation Centre: Gloucester in Gloucestershire
Temporary War Station: Wickford in Essex.
Stations occupied subsequent to Concentration: mobilisation only.

(a) **MOBILISATION.** Units commenced to be formed Jan 29th 1915.

(b) **CONCENTRATION AT WAR STATIONS.** No railway moves, travelled by road to Wickford from Gloucester, June 30 July 2nd 15.

(c) **ORGANISATION FOR DEFENCE.** The picqueting of certain roads as per secret orders & C/35. or amendment ex Hdqrs July 30th 15.

(d) **TRAINING.**

The musketry Courses Parts 1-2-3 as per circular Mar 25th 15 have been completed with satisfactory results. The training of late has been chiefly of an "active service" character. Village skirmishing, road fighting, all night work. Night work is carried out at least once a week. Skeleton forces are always employed. Road patrol work by day & by night, written reports of observations sent back to operation base. Schemes & duties being chiefly based on F.A.1 40 misc

The training of fire control & fire discipline is somewhat 97H handicapped. — all rifles will be returned to Weedon on arrival & chits for same. Rifles at present number 50 for the unit.

(e) **DISCIPLINE.**

The discipline of the unit has been maintained, and is such that the work is carried out with good moral. No complaints have as yet been received for damage in billets, or on operations.
Entries on B.122 are nominal.

WAR DIARY (continued)

(f) ADMINISTRATION.
- Medical services: satisfactory. Capt M.O.
- Veterinary services: not required
- Supply Services: Ex Chelmsford, satisfactory.
- Transport services: daily ex Chelmsford. regular.
- Ordnance services: The delivery of small parts for bicycles has not yet been made, thus necessitating continual local purchases. Otherwise delays are not abnormal, the main thing, an indent not being worked at the moment.
- Billeting & Hutting: No complaints by men, inspections satisfactory.
- Channels of correspondence in routine matters: Headquarters of Division
- Range Construction: ———
- Supply of remounts: ———

(g) REORGANISATION OF T.F. INTO HOME AND IMPERIAL SERVICE.

Unit recruited only imperial service men. 169 S. Alder transferred to 82nd Prov: Co. War Office author: this man refuses to be operated on for incipient appendicitis.

(h) PREPARATION OF UNIT FOR IMPERIAL SERVICE.

The orders of parades have been such as to convey an idea of the actual work likely to be done on active service 7A1 40/974.
Careful medical examinations.
Lectures on notes from the fronts & trench warfare.
Officers & N.C.O. sent to attend lectures and courses as published in Divl: Orders & S.C. Orders.
Great stress being made on the necessity of taking cover, & sanitation at all lectures and on operations.

J. Lancy M Thomas.

Capt. Commanding
61st.(S.M.)Divl.Cyclist Company.

WAR DIARY
of
61st (S.M.) DIVISIONAL CYCLIST CO.

Hour, Place, Date.	Summary of Events and Information	Remarks and References to Appendices
1.12.15. WICKFORD	Field Operations with 60th Divl. Cyclist Co. stopped owing to inclement weather. One man proceeded to School of Farriery WOOLWICH.	H.A.M.
2.12.15 9.a.m. 2:30 p.m.	Company Training Medical Inspection by C.M.O. CAPT. J. LANGDON THOMAS proceeded to Divl. Hdqrtrs. BOREHAM on duty CAPT P.E. DUTTON assumes temporary command of the unit. CAPT. H. INNOCENT 1/8 Cyclist Batln. Essex Regt appointed temporary President of F Area Formation Quartering Committee. CAPT. P.E. DUTTON appointed temporary member of F Area Formation Quartering Committee. Six men reported Back from M. BENFLEET from civil labour. Four men reported here from 3rd Line Depôt. Divl. Cyclist Co. CHELTENHAM and taken on strength of this unit.	H.A.M.

Hour, Place, Date		Summary of Events & Information	Remarks & References to Appendices
3.12.15	WICKFORD	Field Operations with 60th Divl. Cyclist Co. postponed owing to inclement weather.	H.A.W.
4.12.15	9 a.m.	Company Training. 42640 Rfn. .303 S.A.A. (Ball) received from O.O. COLCHESTER.	H.A.W.
5.12.15	9.15 a.m.	Church Parade.	H.A.W.
6.12.15	9 a.m.	Company Training. Six men proceeded to WOOLWICH for Cycle Repairing Course. 42640 Rfn. .303 S.A.A. (Ball) returned to O.O. COLCHESTER.	H.A.W.
7.12.15	9 a.m.	Company Training	H.A.W.

WAR DIARY.

Unit. 1/8th(Cyclist) Bn. Essex Regt.

Division. 61st (South Midland) Division for Administration and Discipline.

Army. Third Army for Operation and Training.

Disposition. Battalion concentrated under canvas on the 28th August, 1915., at "RAWLINGS" 1½ miles W. of SOUTHMINSTER.

Training. The concentration of the Unit has greatly facilitated Battalion training, which has been continued.

General and special work carried out in connection with the Defence of the Peninsula.

Numerous night schemes have also been carried out.

Administration. **Transport.** Fourteen new box-body motor lorries have been supplied by the War Office and twelve old lorries are to be transferred to the Second line Unit.

Ordnance Services. The whole of the bicycles indented for to replace those unserviceable have now been received.

W.F. Ackland

Major,
Commanding 1/8th. (Cyclist) Bn. Essex Regt

Southminster,
12th. September, 1915.

WAR DIARY.

Unit.	1/8th (Cyclist) Bn. Essex Regt.
Division.	61st (South Midland) Division for Administration and Discipline.
Army.	Third Army for Operation and Training.
Disposition.	Battalion concentrated under canvas on the 28th August, 1915., at "RAWLINGS" 1½ miles W. of SOUTHMINSTER.
Training.	The concentration of the Unit has greatly facilitated Battalion training, which has been continued.
	General and special work carried out in connection with the Defence of the Peninsula.
	Numerous night schemes have also been carried out.
Administration.	Transport. Fourteen new box-body motor lorries have been supplied by the War Office and twelve old lorries are to be transferred to the Second line Unit.
	Ordnance Services. The whole of the bicycles indented for to replace those unserviceable have now been received.

W.F. Ackland

Major,
Commanding 1/8th. (Cyclist) Bn. Essex Regt.

Southminster,
12th. September, 1915.

Army Form C. 2118.

November CONFIDENTIAL

WAR DIARY
or
INTELLIGENCE SUMMARY

(Erase heading not required.)

Instructions regarding War Diaries and Intelligence Summaries are contained in F. S. Regs., Part II. and the Staff Manual respectively. Title pages will be prepared in manuscript.

Hour, Date, Place	Summary of Events and Information	Remarks and references to Appendices
1st Wickford	No 2 Sergt Luscombe returned to duty from Billericay	
	225 Cpl Manning proceeded to Billericay	
2nd "	nil	
3rd "	Lt Hall & Lt Margett returned with 14 men from special duty re anti air craft Billericay	
4th Pickmere	3 platoons Field operations (Divisional)	
5th Billericay	Company Brigade field operation	
	Lt O.W. & Sergt Bates returned from course "Field Engineering". Gained certificates good	
Wickford	Sergt Belsher returned to duty with this unit, from alternative centre Slater	
6-10 Wickford	nil	
11th "	3. L.D Stones received from G.H.Q. Elms Ford	
12th "	Field operations cancelled	
13 "	nil	
14 "	1423 Spr Lewis re-engaged S.	
15-21 "	nil	
22 "	2 Lt Hall proceeded to Bisley machine gun course	
	177 Pte Brawton proceeded S to Cookery Depot St Albans	
23 "	nil	
24 "	Six men granted furlough for civilian employment on farm	
25-8 "	nil	
29 "	2270 L/Cpl Miller returned from Sgn Allen's School Dunmow (1st class cert?)	
30 "	No 226 Cpl A.H.James transferred to 3rd Eric Corps R.E. because Home Service Army entered on all A.F.B 178 dental treatment	
	G.W.R.P. Haskell returned to Heron F.Men on 1st class work	

Lieut J. Guildshire Co :- Wickford

Comdr 61 2nd Dist Byfleet R.D
N.C.(C.F)R.D

CONFIDENTIAL.

WAR DIARY of the 61ST (S.M.) DIVL. CYCLIST COY.

FROM 1ST DECR. TO 31ST DECR. 1915.

VOL. 4.

WAR DIARY
of
61st (S.M.) DIVISIONAL CYCLIST CO.

Hour, Place, Date.		Summary of Events and Information	Remarks and References to Appendices
1.12.15.	WICKFORD	Field Operations with 60th Divl. Cyclist Co. stopped owing to inclement weather. One man proceeded to School of Farriery WOOLWICH.	H.A.M.
2.12.15	9.a.m. 2.30 p.m.	Company Training Medical Inspection by C.M.O. CAPT. J. LANGDON THOMAS proceeded to Divl. Hdqtrs BOREHAM on duty CAPT. P.E. DUTTON assumes temporary command of the unit CAPT. H. INNOCENT 1/8 Cyclist Batln. Essex Regt appointed temporary President of F Area Formation Quartering Committee. CAPT. P.E. DUTTON appointed temporary member of F Area Formation Quartering Committee. Six men reported back from N. BENFLEET from civil labour. Four men reported here from 3rd Line Depôt, Divl. Cyclist Co. CHELTENHAM and taken on strength of this unit.	H.A.M.

Hour, Place, Date	Summary of Events & Information	Remarks & References to Appendices
3.12.15 WICKFORD	Field Operations with 60th Divl. Cyclist Co. postponed owing to inclement weather.	A.H.W.
4.12.15 9 a.m.	Company Training. 42640 Rds. .303 S.A.A. (Ball) received from O.O. COLCHESTER.	A.H.W.
5.12.15 9.15 a.m.	Church Parade.	A.H.W.
6.12.15 9 a.m.	Company Training. Six men proceeded to WOOLWICH for Cycle Repairing Course. 42640 Rds. .303 S.A.A. (Ball) returned to O.O. COLCHESTER.	A.H.W.
7.12.15 9 a.m.	Company Training.	A.H.W.

Hour, Place, Date		Summary of Events and Information	Remarks + References to Appendices
8.12.15	9.a.m. WICKFORD	Company Route March. Route WICKFORD - RETTENDON - S.HANNINGFIELD - DOWNHAM - WICKFORD.	M.H.U.
	2.30 p.m.	Medical Inspection by C.M.O. Kit Inspection.	H.H.U.
9.12.15		Company Training	H.H.U.
10.12.15		Company Training	H.H.U.
11.12.15	9.a.m.	Company Route Ride. Route WICKFORD - CRAYS HILL - BILLERICAY - RAMSDEN HEATH - WICKFORD.	
		Eight men reported from 3rd Line Depôt Div. Cyclist Co. CHELTENHAM and taken on strength of this unit.	
12.12.15	9.15 a.m.	Church Parade.	H.H.U.
13.12.15		Company Training One man released for munition work. LIEUT S.A. HALL returned to duty from Machine Gun Course of Instruction BISLEY.	H.H.U.

Hour, Place, Date	Summary of Events to Information	Remarks & References to Appendices
13.12.15 WICKFORD	2/Lieut. B.B. Jack returned to duty from sick leave. S.O.C. inspected Recreation Rooms.	H.M.h.
14.12.15 – 9 a.m.	Company Route March. Route:- WICKFORD – CARPENTERS ARMS – RAWRETH – BATTLESDRIDGE – WICKFORD. 117 Rifles & Bayonets (complete) received from 2/Herts Regt Newmarket.	H.M.h.
15.12.15 – 8 a.m. 2:30 p.m.	Field operations postponed owing to inclement weather. Medical inspection by C.M.O.	H.M.h.
16.12.15	Company Training. One man reported back from cookery course, St ALBANS.	H.M.h.
17.12.15	Company Training	H.M.h.
18.12.15	Company Route Ride. Route:- WICKFORD – NEVENDON – BURNTMILLS – NEVENDON – PITSEA – N.BENFLEET – NEVENDON – WICKFORD.	H.M.h.

Hour. Place - Date		Summary of Events Information	Remarks & References to Appendices
18.12.15	WICKFORD	Six men returned from Cycle Repairing Course, WOOLWICH.	B.B.J.
19.12.15 - 9.30		Church Parade.	B.B.J.
20.12.15		Company Training	B.B.J.
21.12.15		Company Training. Plan of Brian Kiln Pit proposed/linked new Rifle Range submitted & Drill	B.B.J.
22.12.15		Manoeuvres, BOREHAM. Company Training. CAPT. P.E. DUTTON proceeded on leave. LIEUT. A.C. STEWART assumes temporary charge.	B.B.J.
23.12.15		Company Training.	B.B.J.
24.12.15 9am		Company - Route March - Route. WICKFORD - DOWNHAM - RAMSDEN HEATH - RAMSDEN BELL-HOUSE - WICKFORD. 26 Rifles & Bayonets (complete) Received from 2/1 CAMBS. REGT. NEWMARKET.	B.B.J.

Hour. Place. Date		Summary of Events Information	Remarks references & appendices
24.12.15	WICKFORD	57900 Pte. 3033 S.A.A. (See) 2/1. HERTS. REG! NEWMARKET & 200 Rds from 2/4 CAMBS. REG! NEWMARKET.	B.B.J.
25.12.15 9.15 am		Church Parade. The King's Christmas Message to his Navy & Army read to the Unit.	B.B.J.
26.12.15 9.15		Church Parade. Two horses (L.D.) received from N°1 Coy A.S.C. CHELMSFORD.	B.B.J.
27.12.15 9.30 am		Company Rool Call.	B.B.J.
28.12.15		Company Training. Sixteen proceeded to WOOLWICH for Rifle Repairing Course Company Training.	B.B.J.
29.12.15		D.O.R.E. representative arrived at HDQRS to inspect Drier Kiln re proposed Rifle Range (miniature) ONE HORSE (L.D.) transferred 5/2/2 R.F.A. GIBADDOW.	B.B.J.

Name -Place, Date	Summary of Events Information	Remarks & References & Appendices
30.12.15 WICKFORD	Company Training. Rifles & Bayonets cleaned & the C.O.Y	S.S.9.
31.12.15	Brigade Field Day.	182nd Inf. Brigade Order No 30. S.S.9.

A. C. Stewart
Lieut. i/c. 61st S. Midd Divl. Cyclist Co.

CONFIDENTIAL

War Diary of

61st (S.M.) Divisional Cyclist Coy.

from 1st Jany 16. to 31st Jany 1916.

Army Form C. 2118

WAR DIARY
or
INTELLIGENCE SUMMARY
(Erase heading not required.)

Instructions regarding War Diaries and Intelligence Summaries are contained in F.S. Regs., Part II. and the Staff Manual respectively. Title Pages will be prepared in manuscript.

Place	Date	Hour	Summary of Events and Information	Remarks and references to Appendices
Wickford	1.1.15	9am	Company Training.	B.B.J.
	2.1.15	9.15-	Church Parade.	B.B.J.
	3.1.15	9am	Company Training. Four N.C.O's men reported at Danbury to appear before Travelling Medical Board. Result - ONE N.C.O. Class CII, ONE man BI, TWO men BII.	ADMS. 61st S.M.Div.Ref. 3327/MD/15 1.1.16 B.B.J.
	4.1.15	9am 12 noon	Company Training. Inspection by MAJ.GEN.BANNATINE-ALLASON, C.B. Commdg. 61st (S.M.) DIVISION. One man released for demolition work. Southern Command Order No 9 - Saluting read to Company.	W.O. Letter 19/Gen/No 1 54/5 (A.G.1) Released B.B.J. B.B.J.
	5.1.16	9am	Company Training. Southern Command Order No 9 - Saluting read to Company. Civil Land Agent arrived to agree to access claim for damages to back premises.	B.B.J. APPENDIX "A"
	6.1.16	9am	Tactical Exercise. Southern Command Order No 9 - Saluting read to Company.	B.B.J.
	7.1.16	9am 6pm	Company Training. Company Route March - Route - WICKFORD - STOCK Rd - DOWNHAM - LONDON Rd - WICKFORD.	B.B.J.
	8.1.16	9am	Company Rifle Training. Received instructions from 76 dgns. Downham to collect 1000 Rds .303 Blank.	B.B.J.
	9.1.16	9.15-	Church Parade.	B.B.J.

WAR DIARY
or
INTELLIGENCE SUMMARY

(Erase heading not required.)

Army Form C. 2118

Instructions regarding War Diaries and Intelligence Summaries are contained in F.S. Regs., Part II. and the Staff Manual respectively. Title Pages will be prepared in manuscript.

Place	Date	Hour	Summary of Events and Information	Remarks and references to Appendices
WICKFORD	10.1.16	9 am	Board of Survey on Equipment.	Div Order 2284/22/74/c
		2.30	Company Training.	B.S.J.
			Received instructions per Tactical Exercise, Tuesday 11.1.16 from Divl. Engrs - BOREHAM.	
			THREE MEN proceeded to WOOLWICH on Cycle Repairing Course.	
			Received instructions from DIVL HDQRS to move UNIT to BURNHAM.	
	11.1.16	8.15 am	Tactical Exercise.	APPENDIX "B" B.S.J.
		6 pm	Billeting Party left for BURNHAM.	
			ONE N.C.O. returned for Ammunition Work.	W.O. Lester 19/Gen. N⁰ 541S(CA.4.1) Barnes B.S.J.
			FOUR men sent to Cycle Repairing Course, Woolwich.	
	12.1.16	1 pm	Company left WICKFORD by road for BURNHAM.	
		3.30	Company arrived at BURNHAM.	
		10.30	Ammunition Convoy & Guard arrived at BURNHAM.	
			Company billeted at Class II Rate & rations drawn from O/c Supplies, SOUTHMINSTER.	
	13.1.16	9.30	Company Training.	B.S.J.
			ONE man reported back from Farrier Course, Woolwich.	
			Received Instructions from O/C 1/8 CYCLIST BATTLN (ESSEX) REGT to detail Two Anticis for Picquet & Patrol duties, commencing 14.1.16.	
	14.1.16	9 am	Company Training.	B.S.J.

Army Form C. 2118

WAR DIARY
or
INTELLIGENCE SUMMARY
(Erase heading not required.)

Instructions regarding War Diaries and Intelligence Summaries are contained in F.S. Regs., Part II. and the Staff Manual respectively. Title Pages will be prepared in manuscript.

Place	Date	Hour	Summary of Events and Information	Remarks and references to Appendices
WICKFORD	14.1.16	Noon	ONE Officer, TWO N.C.O. & TWENTY ONE men sent to Blackhorne on RIVER CROUCH for patrol duty. ONE Officer, ONE N.C.O. & THREE men sent to LATCHINGTON on Outpost duty.	S.S.J.
	15.1.16	9 am	Company Route March - Route:- Burnham - Ostend - Greekers - Burnham.	B.S.J.
	16.1.16	9.30	Church Parade.	S.S.J.
	17.1.16	9 am	Company Training	S.S.J.
		6 pm	Tactical Route March - Route:- Burnham - Ostend - Burnham	
	18.1.16	9 am	Company Route Ride - Route:- BURNHAM - OSTEND - ALTHORNE - WARDENS FARM - SOUTHMINSTER - BURNHAM.	S.S.J.
		2.30	Company Training CAPT. J. LANGDON THOMAS returned to duty from DIV¹ HD'QRS & resumed command of this unit. One R.A.M.C. N.C.O transferred (attached) returned to his Unit, unfit for foreign Service. Court of Enquiry held to investigate damage to one rifle. Committee for disposal & management of Extra Messing Money formed: - Lieut. A.C. Stewart, Lieut. T.A. Knee, Sheut. J.Z.C. Orr	

WAR DIARY
or
INTELLIGENCE SUMMARY
(Erase heading not required.)

Army Form C. 2118

Place	Date	Hour	Summary of Events and Information	Remarks and references to Appendices
Burnham	19.1.16	9 am	Company Training.	S.S.J.
	20.1.16	9 am	Company Training. Four N.C.O. & men transferred to 82nd Prov¹ Battln & one accordingly struck off strength of this unit. one man returned territorian work. Three men received certificates from Ordnance College Woolwich for repair of Service Bicycles	S.S.J. Reg. O/c Records Auth ⁿᵈ 2116/4/11/16 w/s letter 19 Jan. N⁹ 5415 (A.4.) Releases S.S.J.
	21.1.16	9 am	Company Training Inspection of all rifles by armourer Sergeant. Lieut. Gosling returned to duty, & HEADQUARTERS from BLOCK-HOUSE RIVER CROUCH. BLOCKHOUSE RIVER CROUCH Taken over by senior N.C.O.	
	22.1.16	9 am	Company Training The following Officers reported at HATFIELD PEVERAL from Medical Inspection:- LIEUT. A.C. STEWART - LIEUT. W. GOSLING - LIEUT. S.A. HALL - LIEUT. H. MARGRETT - 2/LIEUT. B. JACK - 2/LIEUT. J.H. ORR.	S.S.J.
	23.1.16	9.30	Church Parade.	S.S.J.

Army Form C. 2118

WAR DIARY
or
INTELLIGENCE SUMMARY
(Erase heading not required.)

Instructions regarding War Diaries and Intelligence Summaries are contained in F.S. Regs., Part II. and the Staff Manual respectively. Title Pages will be prepared in manuscript.

Place	Date	Hour	Summary of Events and Information	Remarks and references to Appendices
BURNHAM	24.1.16	9 am	Company Training. Two N.C.Os proceeded to BISLEY on course of musketry.	B.B.J.
		5 pm	Night operations in conjunction with Rank File - Route - BURNHAM - SOUTHMINSTER - ALTHORNE - OSTEND - BURNHAM.	B.B.J.
	25.1.16	9 am	Company Training.	B.B.J.
	26.1.16	9 am	Company Training.	B.B.J.
		2.30	Medical Inspection by M.O.	
	27.1.16	9 am	Company Training. No 1 Blockhouse (A.B.D) inspected by C.O. & Lieut. S.A. HALL & Coast between No 1 & 2 Blockhouses.	B.B.J.
	28.1.16	9 am	Company Training. Company Route March, Route - BURNHAM - SOUTHMINSTER - BURNHAM.	B.B.J.
	29.1.16		Company Training. Three men received certificates for repair of Service bicycles from Ordnance College, WOOLWICH. Church Parade.	B.B.J.
	30.1.16		LIEUT. W. GOSLING & two N.C.Os detailed to attend Grenadier Course at GODSTONE, commencing 2.2.16.	B.B.J.

Army Form C. 2118

WAR DIARY
or
INTELLIGENCE SUMMARY
(Erase heading not required.)

Instructions regarding War Diaries and Intelligence Summaries are contained in F. S. Regs., Part II. and the Staff Manual respectively. Title Pages will be prepared in manuscript.

Place	Date	Hour	Summary of Events and Information	Remarks and references to Appendices
BURNHAM	31.1.16	9 am	Company Training ONE N.C.O reports from 2/7 ROYAL WARWICKS for duty, bayonet fighting & physical training.	Ref. 9/183 of 29/1/16. L.B.J. J. Langstonthomas Capt. Comdg 61st Divl Cyclist Co

31-1-16.
Burnham-on-Crouch

APPENDIX "A"

Tactical Exercise, 61st (S.M.)
Divl Cyclist Coy, 6.1.16.

Report by Lieut. A.C. STEWART

Ref: ½" O.S. Map - Sheet 30.

General Scheme 6.1.16 - 9 AM.

Enemy has landed at SOUTHEND-ON-SEA & is advancing on WICKFORD. Enemy patrols have been seen in the vicinity of LEIGH - EASTWOOD & ROCHFORD.

Special Idea.

Two Platoons wearing White Hatbands to represent the enemy. Four Platoons are ordered to patrol the line HADLEIGH - RAYLEIGH - HOCKLEY & SOUTH FAMBRIDGE.

Instructions

Defence not to cross line HADLEIGH - RAYLEIGH - HOCKLEY - SOUTH FAMBRIDGE - before 11.30 am.

Attack not to cross line - LEIGH - EASTWOOD - ROCHFORD before 11.30 am.

Area of operations.

NORTH - of RIVER CROUCH.
SOUTH - of LEIGH - PITSEA - LONDON Rd
WEST - PITSEA - NEVENDON.

Progress of Scheme.

Headquarters of defending force was placed at road junction SOUTH of C in CARPENTERS ARMS; subsidiary platoon Hdqrs at first T in TARPOTS & at road junction NORTH of N in HANOVER F^m & patrols were pushed out towards SOUTH FAMBRIDGE - RAYLEIGH & HADLEIGH.

O.C. White force concentrated at D in EASTWOOD & sent TWO sections to make feint attack on defending force S. of SOUTH FAMBRIDGE. This attack was held up without redistribution of defending line. The main attack of whole force was then made on the extreme right of defending line along the road - HADLEIGH - TARPOTS. The defending patrols fell back on TARPOTS where they were reinforced by troops held in reserve on third-class road leading from T in TARPOTS E of NORTH BENFLEET to WICKFORD - RAYLEIGH Road. The attack was repulsed.

Ref: ½" O.S. Map - Sheet 30.   APPENDIX "B"

Tactical Exercise, Tuesday
11.1.16

General Idea

G.O.C. 61st (S.M.) Division on the night 10/11/1/16 bivouacked on line WICKFORD - BILLERICAY; received intimation that a raiding force had been severely handled N.W. of CHELMSFORD & was endeavouring to re-embark at MALDON. O.C. Divl. Cyclists was instructed to furnish information of enemy's movements.

Operation Orders

O.C. Divl. Cyclists at 10.30 am proceeded to occupy the bridges over the stream S of M in DANBURY COMMON, S of Sin GAY BOWERS, S of F in HYDE FARM. This having been accomplished we pushed forward in N.E direction, crossing the main MALDON Road at RUN-SELL GREEN, engaging the enemy's cavalry which retired in the direction of LITTLE BADDOW.

www.ingramcontent.com/pod-product-compliance
Lightning Source LLC
Chambersburg PA
CBHW081505160426
43193CB00014B/2601